T0278196

Easy-to-Follow Tutorials
for Arrangements that Awe

FLOWER ACADEMY

Alexander Campbell

Creator of AC Floral Studio

PAGE STREET
PUBLISHING CO.

PAGE STREET
PUBLISHING CO.

First published in 2024 by
Page Street Publishing Co.
27 Congress Street, Suite 1511
Salem, MA 01970
www.pagestreetpublishing.com

Distributed by Macmillan, sales in Canada by The Canadian Manda Group.

28   27   26   25   24   1   2   3   4   5

ISBN-13: 979-8-89003-125-9

Library of Congress Control Number: 2023948939

Cover and book design by Emma Hardy for Page Street Publishing Co.
Photography by Rafa H. Arteaga

Printed and bound in China

To Queenie

TABLE of

CONTENTS

INTRODUCTION

Handling flowers is the simplest yet most profound way to establish communion with nature. It instills peace and awakens joy. When you make a flower arrangement, you enter into a meditative bubble, completely protected from the worries and anxieties of the external world, and you can live freely and openly as the most authentic version of yourself. You can express yourself however you want. You can find peace within yourself. Nature is nurturing. Nature is healing.

I'm not actually that interested in flowers. What I am interested in, however, is the point in which a flower ceases to be a flower and starts to become color, texture and form. I am interested in the crossroad at which a flower departs from being a sole material and becomes part of a unified whole. I am interested in the cataclysmic moment when a flower stops resembling a flower and takes on a whole other form entirely. I am interested in fleeting, ephemeral moments of beauty that reflect the transitory nature of everything around us. I am interested in the moment when a flower becomes art.

Flower arranging is, at its core, a creative endeavor: As paint is medium to a painter and clay to a ceramicist, flowers and foliage are medium to a florist. As children, we are conditioned to believe that creativity is an impractical, fruitless pursuit, and only in the rarest of cases could it surmount to being something more than a hobby. Responsibility and practicality creep in, and we somehow leave our innate sense of creativity to one side, preferring to focus our efforts on something more materialistically tangible and "useful."

I did, at least. Growing up, I loved being creative. I enjoyed drawing, painting, sewing and generally just using my hands to make things. As a child, I constantly sought approval, and there is one moment that sticks in my mind as the first time I saw pride in the eyes of someone from whom I so desperately sought respect. Sadly, that was a pivotal moment for me. I left my creative pursuits to one side and focused all my efforts on studying harder and harder.

As I waded through my teenage years, my academic efforts took on new meaning: I wanted to leave the small town where I grew up. Being accepted into a good university would be a one-way ticket into the city for good. I graduated in 2018 with first-class honors in Russian and Finnish from University College London (UCL) but felt no clearer about where I wanted to go, who I wanted to be and what I wanted to do. I moved to Spain in 2018 because it had always been a place where I felt my happiest and where I felt I could be the most authentic version of myself. It was during this time that I decided to look into flower arranging. Flowers brought back vivid memories of happy days in my grandmother's garden and spending time with my mum. I decided to take the plunge and study a course in floral design, and I've never looked back.

After setting up my business in Spain, AC Floral Studio has gone from strength to strength, something for which I feel grateful every single day. Finding my passion through creativity has infused my life with a depth and richness I never thought possible. It has allowed me to express myself, not only to people around the world but also to myself: I have discovered countless things about who I am through creating with flowers. I am proud of myself, and I no longer seek external validation for who I am as a person. More important, creativity has given me a profound sense of purpose and gratitude: I know who I am, I like who I am and I know what I am doing. I still don't know where I am going . . . but I've come to realize that the unknown is part of what makes life more enjoyable.

Learning to work with flowers is much more than learning how to put stems in water. In this book, I'm going to teach you how to be a confident, creative and successful florist. Together, we will learn the fundamentals of floral design, from the basic tools you'll need to get started on your journey, to hand-tied bouquets, vase arrangements and large-scale event work. The only things you need to begin are creativity, vision and a dream.

I hope that my book will inspire you to be creative, to reconnect with your soul and to delve deeper into the exciting yet complex labyrinth of who you are as a person.

Alexander Campbell

LAYING ROOTS

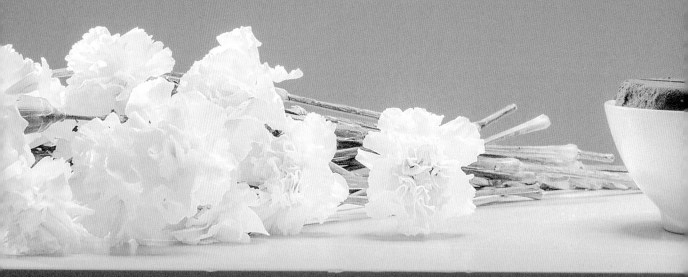

By far, the two most important things you'll need in your floristry toolbox are creativity and a bit of vision. That being said, there are a few other skills that are pretty important for any florist! Understanding how to work with tools will help you properly condition and care for your flowers, in turn creating high-quality floral arrangements. In the following chapter, you'll learn which tools you need and how to properly use them. Later on, our focus turns to design principles and color theory and how adequately employing them can elevate your work into true pieces of art.

Materials and Tools

Let's start at the very beginning—your toolbox! This chapter lists the most important materials and implements you will carry with you as a florist. A note here: Not all of them are necessary for starting out. If you're a hobby florist or simply enjoy decorating your home with arrangements, then some nice blooms, scissors, a knife and some twine will generally suffice. Buy as you go; if you need more tools, consult the following lists. Floristry should never feel overwhelming, and it doesn't have to break the bank.

Flowers

The most frequent question I get asked is, "Where do I source flowers?" You're in luck! For this book, I've tried to use flowers that are commonly available in grocery stores or markets. However, should you want to use more specific flowers, there are a couple of places you can turn to. I always buy my flowers from an online wholesaler, hoekflowers.com, and the flowers arrive at my doorstep the next day if I order before 6:00 p.m. The good thing about online wholesalers is that you can find pretty much every type of flower possible, as they come directly from the Dutch wholesale markets. Even if the wholesaler doesn't have the flower you're looking for in stock, nine times out of ten they can source it for you with a little extra time. The downside to using an online wholesaler is that there is usually a minimum order charge, and sometimes you'll be required to have a business license.

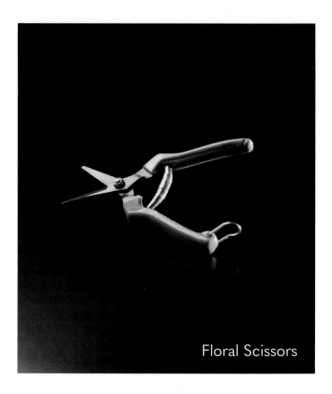

Floral Scissors

Scissors and Knives

Floral Scissors

A good-quality pair of floral scissors is the most important part of your toolbox! Floral scissors, as opposed to normal paper scissors you may have at home, are extra sharp, allowing you to make precise, clean cuts.

Secateurs

Secateurs are heavy-duty scissors for cutting branches and thicker woody stems.

Paper Scissors

Paper scissors are needed for cutting paper, ribbons and string for finishing bouquets.

Wire Cutters

Wire cutters are needed for large-scale event work where wire is needed. Wire cutters are also necessary for working with fake/silk flowers.

Floral Knife

A floral knife is an alternative to floral scissors; floral knives allow you to quickly and easily cut your stems.

Kitchen Knife

A larger knife is mainly used to cut floral foam.

Rose Stripper

A rose stripper is ideal for making your job easier when removing thorns and leaves from roses. To use a stripper properly, start stripping from approximately 4 inches (10 cm) down from the head of your rose. Use gentle movements, working up and down, until all the leaves and thorns are removed and you're left with a clean stem.

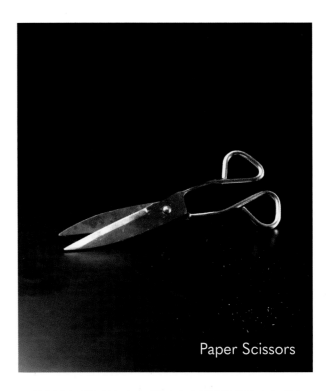

Paper Scissors

Rose Stripper

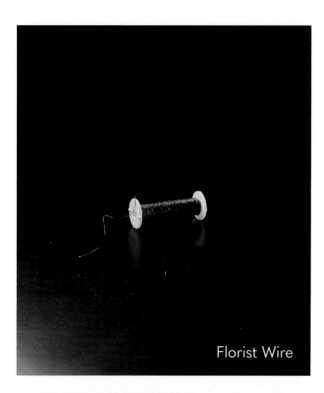

Florist Wire

Adhesives

Floral Tape

Floral tape is a strong, waterproof tape that will hold your mechanisms in place. Floral tape comes in a few different colors, green being the standard.

Hot Glue

That's right! Hot glue really does come in handy in floristry. From attaching mechanisms to making sure your designs don't move, a hot glue gun is a very handy addition to your floral toolbox.

Floral Putty

Floral putty is a strong, waterproof adhesive used to fix floral frogs (an object that holds a bouquet together) and wire and to line vases.

Florist Wire

Florist wire is an indispensable tool to use when trying to keep flowers facing upward or to angle them in a certain direction. It can also be used to secure arrangements and mechanisms. Note the gauge of the wire when determining the use. A higher gauge will be thinner and more flexible, while a lower gauge is thicker and less malleable but will offer more support.

Ribbon

Ribbons are strands of fabric material used to tie bouquet stems together. They can be placed over string or twine for an added aesthetic choice, or they can be more plain and functional.

Ribbon

Floral Foam

Floral foam, for example Oasis, the most trusted brand, keeps flowers firmly in place and allows you a lot of flexibility in your designs. A drawback to floral foam is that once a stem is inserted, it's best not to remove it. Constantly pulling stems out and putting them back in will over-puncture the foam and weaken it, causing your arrangement to fall apart.

Chicken Wire

Similar to floral foam, chicken wire provides a base in which to place your flowers and create designs. It offers more flexibility than floral foam in an arrangement and is more forgiving if you want to remove stems. Chicken wire also offers a more sustainable alternative to floral foam, a single-use plastic, but only if you reuse it. And remember, sustainability is more than just using chicken wire.

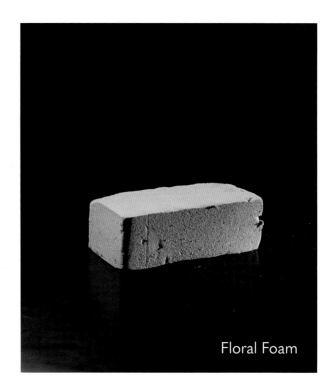

Floral Foam

Flower Care

Once you get your flowers from your wholesaler or provider, you will need to condition them before they are arranged. Conditioning flowers will ensure they are in the best possible condition for the maximum amount of time.

The first thing you'll need to do is remove the outer packaging and remove all the leaves that will fall below the water line. If you are unsure as to where your water line will be, remove all the leaves from the bottom half/bottom two-thirds of the stem. Removing the leaves is so important! As well as making the flower a lot more aesthetic, removing leaves plays a vital role in lengthening flower lifespan. Leaves that sit in the water will rot, releasing harmful bacteria and causing your flowers to wilt much faster.

The next step is to make a very sharp cut on each stem at a 45-degree angle, either with floral scissors or a knife. At this stage, take about 1 inch (2.5 cm) off the bottom of the stem. Cutting at a 45-degree angle creates a larger surface area, allowing for maximum water consumption and preventing stems from lying flat on the bottom of the vase, which would stop them from drinking.

Next, fill your buckets or vases with fresh water and add flower food (see page 16). Make sure your buckets have been cleaned with warm water and a touch of bleach to kill bacteria. Flowers should be left for a few hours (or preferably overnight!) to ensure maximum water consumption before arranging.

Advanced Conditioning Tips

1   Leave flowers out of direct light and in a cool place to ensure maximum shelf life. If you are thinking about opening a flower business, think long and hard about buying a flower fridge. Yes, it can be a big investment for a small business, but it will pay off. Flower fridges lengthen the lifespan of your flowers massively, from a few days to a couple of weeks. If you can't stretch just yet, don't worry—you can leave them in a cool, dark place.

2   For long-lasting hydrangeas, fully submerge the flower bottom-up in water for a few hours/overnight. Hydrangeas are one of the only flowers that drink through their petals as well as through their stem. Submerging them will ensure maximum lifespan and bring back sorry-looking blooms.

3   Woody stems, like hydrangeas, roses, lilac and viburnum need to be cut vertically up the stem for maximum water consumption. After making the first 45-degree cut, make another vertical cut around 1 inch (2.5 cm) up the stem.

4   Some flowers, like amaryllis and delphiniums, have hollow stems. After making your cut, fill the stems with water and block the base with cotton wool.

5   Flower food is always the best option to add to the water to extend the life of your flowers. You can buy all-purpose flower food on Amazon, or at your local florist or plant nursery! If you don't have access to flower food, there are other things you can do. Adding a small amount of vodka to the water will kill any bacteria present. The same goes for a very small amount of bleach or detergent. A spoonful of sugar will also act as flower food and help your blooms stay fresher for longer.

6   Single leaves, for example philodendrons and ferns, can be fully submerged in water before use. This keeps them nice and shiny by removing dust, and ensures that they are fully hydrated.

7   Avoid touching the flower heads too much, as this will weaken them and cause your flowers to wilt faster.

8   Carnations can be opened by gently pressing the base of the flower while gently stroking the petals downward. Never cut carnations on the nodes, always in between them to allow them to drink properly.

9   Roses can be opened either by spinning or "reflexing." Make sure you spin the roses gently for no longer than 10 seconds. To reflex roses, gently flip the outer petals back on themselves. See my full tutorial on page 22.

10 Remove a lily's stamen. The pollen is a nightmare and will stain clothes, furniture and skin.

11 Submerge soft stemmed flowers—such as tulips and anemones—up to their necks for maximum water consumption.

Floristry Techniques

Throughout the book, there will be several floristry techniques that we will repeat time and time again. To make life easier, I've decided to compile the main ones in one comprehensive list here!

Spiral Technique (Bouquet Making)

The spiral technique is the most common and most useful technique in bouquet making. At first it may seem daunting, fiddly and downright annoying! But I promise, it gets easier and actually massively simplifies your life once you get the hang of it. Using the spiral technique allows you to evenly distribute your stems throughout your bouquet, creating a beautiful arrangement. If you're anything like me, the words "uniform" and "evenly" send shivers down my spine. But don't worry! The spiral technique can be used to create both symmetrical and asymmetrical bouquets, so you can still go wild in your designs but do so in a more simplified way.

Here are the steps to create a spiral bouquet:

1   Hold the biggest flower (or your favorite flower) in your hand. This will become the focal point of your bouquet—you're going to be laying all subsequent stems around it.

2 Position a couple of smaller flowers at an angle on top of your feature flower in your hand.

3 Holding the flowers loosely, turn the baby bouquet 180 degrees.

4 Add another "feature" flower (generally, a large, beautiful bloom that has a lot of impact!), placing it at an angle on top of the other stems.

5 Hold the bouquet loosely and turn. The flowers are going to jiggle around, and that's okay! You can pull them back up again and encourage them to stay where you put them in the first place. Don't get frustrated, you can do this!

6 Continue adding flowers and stems of foliage, holding the bouquet loosely, and turning your arrangement as you go.

7 When all your flowers have been used up, take time to pull some stems out, and push some stems in, creating height, depth and interest.

8 Tie the stems tightly with ribbon or twine.

9 Cut the stems to your desired length.

And ta-da! That's it. Your first spiral bouquet.

Painting Natural Materials

Spray painting foliage, leaves and flowers is a perfect way to color-match your materials and to get the exact tone you need. A note here: Try not to use too many painted materials in one arrangement! From experience, more than one or two painted elements feels too false and massively detracts from the flowers.

To paint natural materials, you'll need to use a water-based spray paint. Make sure you've fully conditioned your stems first (see page 15). Now, it's time to paint! Shake the can well. Holding the can 6 to 12 inches (15 to 30 cm) away, aim directly at your materials and spray until everything is covered evenly. Leave your materials to dry in a well-ventilated room, or better still, outside. I always paint on my terrace, and I have a special painting bucket that I leave stems to stand in. Sometimes, you'll need to do two coats of paint, but I only do this if I'm using a very light color paint on a dark colored leaf.

Tying Bouquets

There are lots of ways to tie flowers, but I'm going to share with you my favorite way to tie them! It will make your life so much easier, I promise.

1   Cut a long length of thread or twine 16 to 20 inches (40 to 50 cm) long; I always prefer to give myself plenty to work with.

2   Make a loop with the twine so that both ends are of equal length.

3   After finishing your bouquet, lay the loop over the stems, open the loop with your free hand and pull the other side through, creating a tight hold.

4   Holding one end, send the other end all the way around the bouquet, pulling tightly.

5   With both ends at the front again, pull tightly.

6   Finally, tie both ends in a knot.

7   Cut the ends to your desired length (I prefer to cut them short and use a longer ribbon for decoration).

Before

After

Reflexing Roses

In several of the projects to follow, I've reflexed the roses. It takes an otherwise uninspiring rose and turns it into a completely different, fully Instagram-worthy bloom. Here's how to do it.

1   Begin by turning your rose upside down and spin the stem quickly between your hands for around 10 seconds. This will loosen up the bloom and help you to open up the petals.

2   Remove the outer guard petals (these will be the uglier, probably torn petals!).

3   Start by gently folding the petals, one by one, over your forefinger with your thumb. Roses are fragile, so go slowly but surely.

4   Repeat this step around the bottom third to half of the bloom. It's best to leave some stems folded up to give the rose a more natural feel.

Using Floral Foam

We will be using floral foam in several projects throughout the book. Floral foam holds the flowers in place, and it acts as a water source for them.

But how do we use it? Well, the good news is that it isn't very difficult! First, fill your sink or a large bucket with water, drop your floral foam on top of the water and simply let it sink! This should take 2 to 3 minutes. It is really important not to push your floral foam down, as this will only wet the outside and the inside will be completely dry,

meaning your flowers will not be able to drink. (There is something tragically poetic about this and reminds me of the Greek mythological figure Tantalus, who was submerged in water for all eternity, but forever denied the pleasure of drinking, leaving him in a constant state of thirst.)

Once sunk, carefully take the floral foam out of the water (it will now be considerably heavier!), shake off any excess water, and you're good to use it in your projects. Once floral foam is soaked, it can't absorb any more water, so no need to add any more water to the block once it's placed in your arrangement.

Fundamental Design Principles

Before I became a florist, I thought all flower arrangements were wonderful: the ones I saw on Pinterest, the ones my mum made with flowers from her garden and even the ones I would buy from the supermarket on a weekend morning. However, since becoming a florist, that infatuation with all florals has become somewhat skewed. I find myself overly critical of flower choices that are put together for mass-sale at the grocery store, and nowadays I don't automatically save every photo I see. But what changed?

In essence, I think it boils down to this: Flowers grouped together are always going to be lovely simply because the raw material is pleasing. However, flowers that are properly arranged in accordance to a certain set of "design rules" cease to be merely aesthetic and have the power to become true works of art. And this is the difference. Now, working as a florist, my eye automatically looks for balance, for symmetry, for line and for harmony. And when something is missing, the beauty of the raw material is simply not enough to raise my appreciation to a level of true infatuation.

I don't want my words to be misconstrued here—flowers in themselves always have been lovely, and they always will be lovely. I will never not appreciate them. However, by understanding the main design principles in floristry—balance, scale, proportion, emphasis, contrast, rhythm and harmony—your appreciative eye can become an artist's tool, a hand with which you will compose true floral masterpieces.

The following principles will help you create physically and visually stunning arrangements.

Balance

In design, there are two types of balance: physical and visual. Physical balance in floristry refers to the even distribution of materials so that one side of the arrangement isn't heavier or more loaded than the other. Visual balance refers to how symmetrical, or asymmetrical, an arrangement is.

Scale

Scale refers to how any given arrangement interacts with its surroundings. For example, a large urn arrangement is more suited to a church than it is to a studio apartment. Scale is also implicit of color and texture, and how they are combined to create a gradual scale from one end of the spectrum to the other.

Proportion

While scale looks at how the arrangement reacts with external factors, proportion studies how different elements within the arrangement react with one another. This could be the balance of height and width or the proportion of flowers to the container.

Emphasis

Emphasis refers to the focal point of an arrangement. This could be a big "star" flower that grabs your attention, or it could be a strong color contrast. It becomes one of the most important visual parts of an arrangement.

Contrast

A successful contrast supports its design brother emphasis, helping to highlight an important flower or part of an arrangement. Similar to emphasis, contrast can be achieved through a strong visual color combination, flower choice or textural elements.

Rhythm

Rhythm refers to the overall flow of the arrangement. The eye is drawn to an emphatic central element, and then guided harmoniously through the rest of the arrangement. Not only does this add movement, but it also helps to focus the viewer's attention on the point you most want to emphasize.

Harmony

Harmony, quite unsurprisingly, refers to how harmonious and balanced the overall arrangement is. Harmony takes into account these seven guiding principles, along with your choice of color, texture and flower, and it is achieved when they all work in perfect tandem to create something visually appealing.

The Color Wheel

Color Theory

Fundamental to becoming a proficient florist is a solid understanding and appreciation of color theory. Color theory is both an art and a science. It dictates how we experience colors, explains how colors, tones and hues mix and has the power to communicate messages and ideas.

Color theories create a logical structure for color and our understanding of it. Color is organized on the color wheel, which is divided into three categories: primary colors, secondary colors and tertiary colors.

Why is it so important to understand color theory in floristry? Well, color has the incredible power to convey not only messages, but emotions, feelings and sentiments. An understanding of color theory will help you to create harmonious and visually impactful arrangements. Let's see how it works!

The Color Wheel

The color wheel simplifies the process of understanding color theory for us (phew!). The color wheel is divided into **three primary colors** (red, yellow, blue), **three secondary colors** (colors that you get from mixing the primary colors—these are green, purple and orange) and **six tertiary colors** (these are made from mixing both primary and secondary colors, for example blue-green or red-pink).

If you slice your color wheel in half vertically, you'll see your **warm colors** (yellows, reds, oranges and pinks) on one side and **cool colors** (blues, greens, purples) on the other.

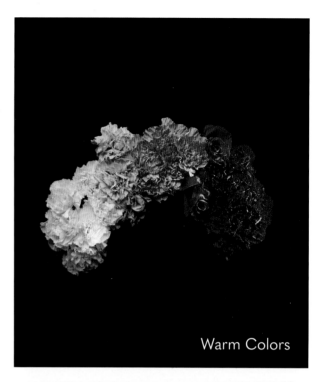

Warm Colors

Cool Colors

Tint

Shade

Tone

Tints, Shades and Tones

Tints, shades and tones further amplify the range of colors. Simply put, tints, shades and tones are all variations of colors on the color wheel. To create a **tint**, we add white. For example, blue + white = sky blue. To create a **tone**, we add black. For example, blue + black = navy blue. To create a **shade**, we add gray. A tone softens and reduces the intensity of color while making the color darker.

Color Schemes

The color wheel helps us to see three different color schemes: complementary colors, analogous colors and triadic colors.

Complementary colors sit directly opposite each other on the color wheel, for example blue and orange or yellow and purple. Complementary colors create strong combinations, as the colors heavily contrast with one another. **Analogous colors** sit next to each other on the color wheel, for example, purple, blue-purple and blue. An analogous scheme creates a softer contrast in design work. And finally, **triadic colors** are three colors evenly placed around the color wheel, for example yellow, blue and red. Triadic color schemes are bold and dynamic color palettes.

A final word on color theory: Use of color, taste and design are inherently subjective, and what may seem abhorrent to one person may be perfect for another. Using color proficiently takes time, effort and practice; however, it is always important to use color authentically and follow your heart. If you like the combination of a blend of warm and cool colors, go for it. Never design or play with color in a certain way because you think you have to instead of wanting to.

Complementary Colors

Triadic Colors

HAND-TIED BOUQUETS

Hand-tied bouquets are a cornerstone of your floral career. For many, they represent the best and worst of floristry. Nightmarishly cumbersome at first, hand-tied bouquets can cause feelings of angst, frustration and loathing. I've been there! When I went to flower school, I hated making bouquets. Now, somewhat paradoxically, I am known in large part for making bouquets and have come to love them. With a little practice, making bouquets becomes easy through the repetitive nature of the task. In the following tutorials, I'm going to show you different ways of holding your stems, and I'll help you find what works best for you. It's a little like riding a bike or learning to knit: After a couple of frustrated attempts, you'll have a breakthrough and eventually be able to do it with your eyes closed.

One thing you can do is go to your local supermarket and buy a cheap bouquet of flowers. Un-make the bouquet and lay your flowers on a table, then remake it. Un-make it and repeat the process. I was told to do this when I was at flower school and did so ten times with the same bouquet. After the sixth or seventh attempt, it started to get easier. Practice makes progress. Rome wasn't built in a day, and perfection doesn't exist. You'll get there.

The following chapter will look into the various ways of making hand-tied bouquets and (I promise) by the end of this chapter, you'll love making them!

CROSSING the RIVER STYX

Crossing into the murky underworld of dark arrangements, we are going to start with a striking black bouquet that is perfect for any occasion. In monochromatic arrangements with less color variety like this one, scale and proportion are of paramount importance. As we make the bouquet together, we will be playing with height and depth as well as texture and size to create as much visual interest as we can. You can get a refresher on these design principles on page 24.

The first time I ever saw a black rose, my heart skipped a beat. It was so beautiful, so elegant, yet also so dark and mysterious. In that moment, my understanding of flowers was completely inverted: Black flowers maintained the beauty and poise of other flowers, but they added something much darker, brooding and occult without looking faded or moribund. Black flowers can be quite difficult (but not impossible!) to come by, and chances are that you will have to order them specially from your supplier or local florist.

This bouquet also seamlessly weaves together natural and spray-painted materials. I use Oasis Easy Color Spray, but any water-based spray paint will do. Coin at the ready, all aboard!

Foliage

2 bunches of ruscus
5–10 corylus branches

Flowers

12 Black Baccara rose stems
10 Black Pearl lisianthus stems
10 Odessa calla lily stems

Supplies

Floral scissors or knife
Black water-based spray paint
Twine
Black ribbon

For a visual glossary of the flowers and foliage used, see the Flower Glossary on page 136. For alternatives, consult the Substitution List (page 138).

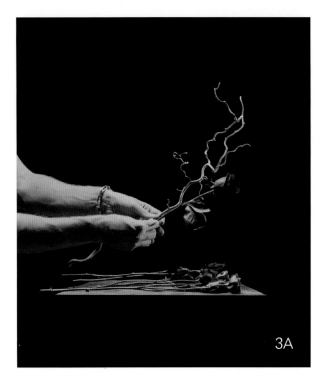

3A

3B

1   Before you start making your arrangement, make sure to carefully condition all your materials (see page 15). Take time to carefully remove any wilted petals and cut the stems with your floral scissors at a 45-degree angle.

2   In a well-ventilated area, spray paint your ruscus leaves. Aim the can directly at the leaves from 6 to 12 inches (15 to 30 cm) away, and lightly spray each leaf until covered in a layer of black. To brush up on painting natural materials, see page 20.

3   When all your foliage is prepped, painted and completely dried, you're ready to go. We're going to start our bouquet with a real showstopper: our Black Baccara roses. Hold one stem together with a piece of painted ruscus and corylus branch in one hand, and then pick a smaller flower, for example the Black Pearl lisianthus. Add the lisianthus in at an angle. Next, add another stem of foliage at an angle, while holding your bouquet. Give the flowers a little turn with your other hand, and grip tightly again. This is the starting point for a spiraling technique, one of the most used, and useful, techniques in floristry (see page 17).

4   Continue to lay the stems in at an angle while twisting your flowers—one rose, two foliage, one calla lily, two foliage, one lisianthus, two foliage—until you run out of flowers. As the bouquet gets larger it will, somewhat paradoxically, get both easier to hold and easier to add flowers into. If you want to make a smaller bouquet, you can stop adding flowers at any point in the process when you find the fullness to your liking and move on to the next steps.

5   Once all the flowers have been added, or the bouquet reaches your desired fullness, adjust your stems. At this point, it is completely normal for your bouquet to look a little flat. One of the many benefits of a spiral bouquet is that you can easily pull out and push in stems. Take time to pull some flowers out, playing with height and depth. You could try adding some foliage toward the lower part of the arrangement or placing some stems at the back of the bouquet. Try lifting the roses out of the foliage by 1 or 2 inches (2.5 to 5 cm) and see if it opens up the design. There is no exact way of doing this, as taste and aesthetic is undeniably subjective and will vary from person to person. But what you should be ultimately aiming for is a bouquet that "breathes." Your flowers should not be clumped together on one level, nor should they all be shooting out at every angle. They should look intentional, like they've always been there, growing happily together in your beautiful midnight garden.

7

6   Once you have the flowers and foliage in the positions you want them, add in your final details—the remaining corylus branches. Go wild here—create height, offshoots and drama. Try adding in a couple of really tall branches toward the back, then some shorter ones at the front. Once added, you can continue to pull out some stems, following the new lines created by the addition of the branches.

7   Gently place your bouquet down on a table and make a tight knot with twine (to learn more about twine-tying skills, see page 20).

8　Gently hold your masterpiece at the base and cut the stems evenly with your floral scissors. The closer you hold your stems to where you want to cut them, the more even and uniform the base will be.

9　Cut a length of black ribbon that is 12 to 20 inches (30 to 50 cm), then tie it neatly around your original knot in a bow (for more on tying ribbons, see page 20). And voila! That's it. Time to pay Charon a coin for safe passage.

The BRIGHT SNOW WHISPERED

For much of human history, there has been an intrinsic link between white and the notions of cleanliness and purity. As the total absence of color, white also represents nothingness. But how can something be nothing? Does that mean the lightness of a feather, which is nothing, is also something? Or the color of water, which is a color, yet also isn't a color? In the following arrangement, we will be creating a dazzling white bouquet, one that is clean, pure and something yet at the same time nothing. As light as a feather, as colorless as water.

This is a foliage-free bouquet, meaning we need to substitute our greenery with something. Enter the hydrangea! Hydrangeas are a fantastic base for dome bouquets like this one, as they provide great support and body. However, this is all they will be; the aim here will be to completely cover them.

A quick note: This bouquet has a more bridal feel and can be made in multiple different color schemes, all of which will transform the bouquet quite drastically. Follow your heart, play around with different colors and make a bouquet that is uniquely yours.

Flowers

2 white hydrangeas
1 packet of white roses
1 packet of white carnations
1 packet of white astilbe
1 packet of white Limonium
1 packet of white veronica
1 packet of white spray roses

Supplies

Floral scissors or knife
Twine
Ribbon (optional)

For a visual glossary of the flowers and foliage used, see the Flower Glossary on page 136. For alternatives, consult the Substitution List (page 138).

1 Before you start making your arrangement, make sure to carefully condition all your materials (see page 15). Take time to carefully remove any wilted petals and cut the stems with your floral scissors at a 45-degree angle.

2 Start by putting two white hydrangeas together. If you have really large hydrangeas, you may want to trim your hydrangeas down to a more manageable size. To do this, flip your hydrangea over and, very carefully, start pruning away parts of the bloom that you deem unnecessary or unsightly. You might be thinking: Why can't I just use one large hydrangea instead of two smaller ones? Honestly, I really have no steadfast answer to this! Two hydrangeas always look better, and I can't put my finger on exactly why.

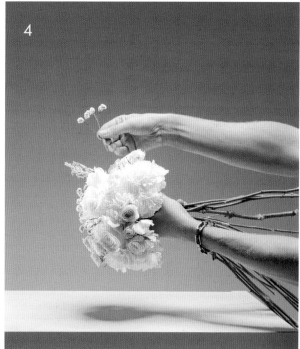

3   This is going to be a relatively symmetrical bouquet, so when adding in your flowers make sure you're looking at the bouquet top-down. Start by adding in your biggest flowers, in our case here, the white roses. The stem needs to directly pierce the hydrangea, seeking space between petals to enter. Go gentle here—hydrangeas are very fragile.

4   Next, add in the carnations. Again, space them symmetrically around the hydrangeas next to the roses, making sure you have some on top of the hydrangea, some at the sides and some lower down. We're looking for an even placement. Now, add in the astilbe. I use three stems—one on the right and two on the left, all slightly off-center. This will add dimension to your bouquet. At this point, I will also usually add little sprigs of Limonium into the center to break up the uniformity and one-dimensionality of the bouquet too.

5   Add in the veronica, following the lines of the astilbe, but slightly lower down. Next, add in the spray roses. Finish off by adding a "skirt" of Limonium around the base of the hydrangeas. This will even out the bouquet. If you think it needs it, add some more Limonium to the center of the arrangement too.

6   As this bouquet has a more bridal feel, we will cut the stems short. Cut a long length of twine and tie off your bouquet (for tying bouquets, see page 20). Measure two hands on the stems and evenly cut the bottoms. You can either leave your bouquet as is or finish it off with a ribbon of your choice.

COUNTRY CLUB

I'm not a huge fan of using foliage in bouquets. I understand why we use it—it's cheap and fills up a lot of space—but I think it detracts a lot from the colors of the arrangement and just adds too much visual noise. So, how to create a green bouquet without actually using greenery? That is the challenge. For this bouquet, I've used lots of different textural stems—for example, tufty dianthus and heavy-headed viburnums—tied together with soft whites to create a harmonious bouquet filled with soothing green tones.

Flowers

1 packet of snowberries (or 1 packet of white hypericum)
1 packet of white trachelium
1 packet of green dianthus
1 packet of Queen Anne's lace
1 packet of green viburnums
1 packet of white dahlias

Supplies

Floral scissors or floral knife
Twine

For a visual glossary of the flowers and foliage used, see the Flower Glossary on page 136. For alternatives, consult the Substitution List (page 138).

1   Before you start making your arrange-
    ment, make sure to carefully condition
    all your materials (see page 15). Take time
    to carefully remove any wilted petals and
    cut the stems with your floral scissors at a
    45-degree angle.

2   Start by holding a stem or two of snowber-
    ries in one hand. These stems are heavy
    and seasonal, so feel free to replace them
    with a long stem of white hypericum.

3   For this bouquet, we're going to be using
    the spiral technique. (To brush up on how
    to do a spiral bouquet, see page 17.) Hold-
    ing the snowberries in your hand, add in
    a single stem of trachelium at a 45-degree
    angle. Grip the two stems gently and turn.
    Add in another two stems of trachelium at an
    angle, together with a stem of snowberries.

4   To add some body to the bouquet, I've chosen to use Queen Anne's
    lace and dianthus. Add a couple of dianthus stems down low. Next,
    add in a couple of stems of viburnum. Viburnums are naturally very
    "floppy" flowers, and they add great movement to arrangements.
    Angle the stems upward so that they hang gently over the other flow-
    ers. Add one Queen Anne's lace stem into the bouquet at an angle,
    gripping gently and turning.

5

5   While turning, add in a dahlia. Holding gently, turn the bouquet once more. Add in another dahlia directly opposite the first one. Sometimes it can help to make a spiral bouquet by looking at it from above. We want an even placement of blooms. For example, if one dahlia is at 12 o'clock, I might add another at 3 o'clock, another at 6 o'clock, and one more at 9 o'clock. By looking at the bouquet from above, I can see if symmetry and even placement has been achieved.

6   Continue the bouquet by adding in the rest of the flowers: one stem of dianthus, one dahlia, turn. One stem of trachelium, one stem of snowberries, turn. Two viburnum, one Queen Anne's lace, turn, until all of the blooms have been exhausted.

7   At this point, your bouquet may be looking a little flat, a little confused or a little messy. Or it may not! In which case, good for you! Mine are usually looking somewhat frazzled and lackluster at this point in the process, but perfection is never very far away. Sometimes all your bouquet needs is a little depth and movement, which are easily achieved by pulling out a few stems and pushing a few in. Other times, your bouquet may look too flat because everything is sitting on the same level, and you can see too many stems. If this happens, try adding in a couple more blooms lower down around the base. It'll add depth and dimension!

8   Finish by tying off the bouquet with twine (to practice the best tying technique, see page 20). And that's it! An elegant and crisp green bouquet.

CHAMPAGNE POWDER

One of my dreams is to go skiing in Colorado. I've never been. The air must be cold and biting, but I can imagine how the Rockies twinkle glee-fully under a lazy winter sun. They say that the term "Champagne Powder" was coined in the '50s by a local ranger who, inhaling the snow, found the sensation to be similar to that of champagne bubbles. The snow is light, dry and smooth, perfect for skiing.

Drawing upon such imagery, we will be using spray-painted materials and pure white flowers, slalomed together to create an arrangement that is as light, as dry and as smooth to the eye as the champagne powder of Colorado.

Foliage

1 packet of ruscus
A few branches of salix

Flowers

1 packet of baby's breath
1 packet of Limonium
1 packet of white dahlias
1 packet of white roses
1 packet of white spray roses
1 packet of white carnations

Supplies

Floral scissors or knife
Metallic silver spray paint
Snow spray (any type from Amazon will do fine!)
Twine
White ribbon (optional)

For a visual glossary of the flowers and foliage used, see the Flower Glossary on page 136. For alternatives, consult the Substitution List (page 138).

1   After conditioning all your flowers and foliage, paint your greenery (see more on conditioning and painting flowers on pages 15 and 20). Here, I have chosen ruscus for its versatility and durability, and for the fact that the leaves are neither too big nor too small. To prepare the ruscus, I take most of the leaves off the stem, leaving only the top three or four. In a well-ventilated area, spray paint your ruscus leaves with the metallic silver spray paint. Aim the can directly at the leaves from 6 to 12 inches (15 to 30 cm) away, and lightly spray each leaf until covered in a layer of silver. Spray your salix and baby's breath with snow spray. Go heavy here. With snow spray, less is not more, more is! Set your foliage aside to dry for a few hours.

2   For this bouquet we will be working in the spiral. If you need a quick refresh on the spiraling technique, see page 17. Start by gathering your salix in a bunch and picking up your tallest Limonium stem. I've chosen salix because they are lightweight and have thin stems and plenty of movement. However, you can add in any branches you want.

3   Give the flowers a little turn and continue adding Limonium. The first Limonium stem will mark our highest point. When adding in flowers, never go higher than this. Hold that stem and add in a piece of painted ruscus.

4   Gripping the flowers, turn them a bit and add Limonium in one hand, and then pick a smaller flower, like a dahlia. Add the dahlia in at an angle. Next, add another painted ruscus at an angle, while holding your bouquet. Give the flowers a little turn with your other hand and grip gently again.

5   Continue to add in flowers, turning the bouquet every stem or so, until you have an even placement of flowers. It doesn't matter which order you add them in, but interchange between adding one rose, spray rose, carnation and sprig of baby's breath. "Finished" is decidedly subjective; perhaps you prefer a more minimalistic bouquet with fewer flowers, or maybe you're like me and think that more is always more! When you get to a size and shape that feels good to you, it's time to stop adding flowers. I will usually use up all of my blooms and then decide that I'm done! Now it will be imperative to pull some stems toward you, and push some back in, to create a three-dimensional piece. This will create depth and movement, ultimately creating a much more natural-feeling arrangement.

6   Finally, tie off your bouquet with twine, and if you like, a nice white ribbon. To brush up on tying bouquets, check page 20.

POSEIDON'S PURSUIT

On the island of Naxos in Greece, Amphitrite, a Nereid, performs a dance. His heart ablaze with desire, the enamored Poseidon asks for Amphitrite's hand in marriage, a request she steadfastly refuses, fleeing to Atlas at the farthest end of the ocean. Not giving up on Amphitrite, Poseidon sends a dolphin in pursuit of her, which manages to convince her to wed Poseidon. In gratitude, Poseidon makes the dolphin into a constellation, to be admired for all eternity.

The following arrangement is based on this myth, using vivid blues and striking gold elements to weave together a floral tale of love and pursuit.

Foliage

1 packet of ruscus

Flowers

10 blue delphinium stems
1 packet of white baby's breath
10 white delphinium stems

Supplies

Floral scissors or floral knife
Metallic gold spray paint
Twine

For a visual glossary of the flowers and foliage used, see the Flower Glossary on page 136. For alternatives, consult the Substitution List (page 138).

2

1   After conditioning all your flowers and foliage, paint your ruscus (see more on conditioning and painting flowers on pages 15 and 20). In a well-ventilated area, aim the spray paint can directly at the leaves from 6 to 12 inches (15 to 30 cm) away, and lightly spray each leaf until covered in a layer of gold. Here, I have chosen ruscus for its versatility and durability, and for the fact that the leaves are neither too big nor too small. To prepare the ruscus, I take most of the leaves off the stem, leaving only the top three or four. Set your foliage aside to dry for a few hours.

2   Start by holding a blue delphinium in your hand. Make sure it's quite straight and tall with an even placement of blooms—this is going to be our center point. Then, take a few cuttings of baby's breath and surround the stem, spiraling as you go. (To refresh your memory on how to make a spiral bouquet, see page 17.) Take three more blue delphiniums and place them evenly around your central stem, working in the spiral. For this bouquet, we are starting at the highest point and working our way down, so the stems need to sit slightly lower than the first stem.

4

5

3 Follow up with another layer of baby's breath. For a wider, more open bouquet, add more baby's breath. For a smaller, tighter bouquet, add fewer. I find that somewhere between the two is the sweet spot.

4 Take four more stems of blue delphinium and repeat the previous step. Add one final layer of baby's breath.

5 Take one stem of white delphinium and place it directly next to your highest point. Here, you have a choice: Either go slightly higher than your original center point or go slightly lower. Imagine these white stems as highlights. They will bring out the best of the blue delphiniums and add tonality and depth to the bouquet.

7

6   Bearing the previous step in mind, highlight your other delphinium stems by adding in white delphiniums near them, always positioning the stems slightly higher or slightly lower than the blue ones.

7   Now, we're going back to the ruscus! Add a skirt of your metallic foliage around the base of the bouquet, evenly placing the stems around it. If you want, you can intersperse the remaining delphiniums with more painted ruscus to intensify the gold element. When you're happy with your golden elements, tie off your bouquet with twine. To brush up on how to tie bouquets, see page 20.

And that's it! Perhaps this arrangement won't light up the skies for all eternity, but it will definitely light up your life with sparkle and joy for a week or so.

AN EVENING IN LATE AUGUST

If ever there was a competition to find a winner amongst all the times of the year, the period when August hands herself into September would forever take the crown. Long days, short nights, but with a cool breeze as autumn takes her first bite. In the garden, August is one of the most vibrant and busy times: flowers bloom, flowers wilt, leaves very gently start to turn orange as September begins. The following arrangement is inspired by this crossroads of seasons, weaving together all the colors and textures that this period brings with it into a stunning bouquet bursting with life and color.

This is a very ingredient-heavy bouquet, I know! But in reality, it isn't a very complicated arrangement to make. As with some of the other bouquets in this book, we're going to be using the spiral technique, a key concept in floral design.

Flowers

1 packet of brown hydrangeas
1 packet of pink hypericum
1 packet of pink spray roses
1 packet of safflowers
1 packet of allium
1 packet of clematis
1 packet of scabiosa pods

Foliage

1 packet of ruscus
1 packet of leucadendron

Supplies

Floral scissors or floral knife
Metallic gold spray paint
Twine

For a visual glossary of the flowers and foliage used, see the Flower Glossary on page 136. For alternatives, consult the Substitution List (page 138).

2

1 After conditioning all your flowers, paint your foliage (see more on conditioning and painting flowers on pages 15 and 20). Begin by spray painting the ruscus gold. In a well-ventilated area, spray paint the leaves. Aim the can directly at the leaves from 6 to 12 inches (15 to 30 cm) away, and spray each leaf until covered in a gleaming metallic layer.

2 Start by holding two brown hydrangeas together. Hydrangeas naturally tilt to one side, so make sure you tilt them into each other. They will look a little scrunched together at first, but trust me! It'll work itself out. Working in a spiral (for more on the spiral technique, see page 17), add in a few stems of deep red leucadendron leaves, spacing them evenly throughout the bouquet. At this stage, start to introduce some gold foliage too.

3A

3B

3 Once the base is built out with hydrangeas and foliage, we can start to add in the flowers. I'm starting with bright pink hypericum, spacing it out evenly throughout the bouquet. Then, add in the pink spray roses. Try to angle these slightly higher up than the other flowers to introduce height and movement into the arrangement.

4 Once all stems are arranged, add in the safflower. To create further movement and texture, I'm adding in these stunning allium flowers. Did you know that these are actually the flowers that onions produce?! If you cut the stems and smell, you'll notice right away. Make sure that the alliums are spread evenly throughout the hydrangea and are currently sitting higher up than all other flowers.

5 If at this point your bouquet looks absolutely nothing like the one in the photo, don't worry! This is completely normal, and you're nowhere near finishing. When I was at flower school, I used to get so desperate at this point that I would want to throw in the towel, walking off in a stomp and saying, "I can't do it." A teacher once told me that if you look at yourself halfway through getting a haircut, you're going to think that you look dreadful. But 15 minutes later you're transformed and you look beautiful. The same goes for flower arrangements. Stick with it and don't give up just yet. Try pulling some blooms out, re-emphasizing your star flowers. Push some in. Play with height, depth and dimension. You may want to take some elements out altogether! Continue until you are happy with the size, shape and dimensions.

6   As a final touch, add in the clematis and scabiosa pods, dancing above the rest of the flowers. They will add a lightness to an otherwise ingredient-heavy bouquet and help to lift the arrangement (take a peek at the photo on page 58 for a visual of this).

7   Keeping your stems long, tie them off with twine (see more on tying your bouquet on page 20). Cut the stems; they should be kept to the length of two or three hands. And voila! A late summer garden, enshrined in a bouquet.

VASE ARRANGEMENTS

The exact origins of using flowers decoratively remain murky. The moment in which organic material transitioned from countryside to hearth has been lost to the annals of time due to insufficient written historical accounts. However, the earliest pictorial data of floral design can be traced back to the Egyptians, around 2500 BC, when flowers were ceremoniously placed in vases. Throughout the ages, flowers remained a constant in religious ceremonies the world over, before experiencing a boom in widespread usage during the Renaissance.

Learning how to properly arrange a vase is an imperative part of your floral journey. Vases, containers and styles may change, but the structures and techniques you use to arrange them will always remain the same. In the following chapter, we will be creating both freestanding vase arrangements (without any supports or mechanisms) and arrangements that use chicken wire or tape to give them structure and support.

63

CAPE COD

October 13, 2019, 6:20 a.m. Jetlagged, I wake up in the sleepy town of Chatham on Cape Cod. The early morning rays of light peep through the white shutters as I lie in bed. I decide to get up and greet the day by taking a walk along Chatham Beach. I wander down past the perfect houses with their gardens full of heavy-headed hydrangeas. Deserted, the beach is perfect as the lazy autumn sun lifts her head above the horizon. Sitting on the beach, looking out at the waves, an enormous sense of gratitude washes over me. Both the Massachusetts morning and my body are still working together in perfect synchrony. Since that morning, Cape Cod has been one of my favorite places on earth.

The following project is inspired by my trips to Cape Cod, drawing inspiration from the colors and textures of the Atlantic Coast of the United States. This is an exceedingly easy arrangement, yet its ease does not compromise its visual impact. The mix of delphiniums in different shades and hues adds great depth, lending the arrangement a varied, nuanced appeal. This same arrangement could also work with only one color, but the overall effect would, obviously, be significantly different.

Flowers

5 blue hydrangeas
1 packet white Limonium or baby's breath
1 packet dark blue delphinium
1 packet white delphinium

Supplies

Floral scissors or a floral knife
A clear glass vase (12 to 20 inches [30 to 50 cm] in height)

For a visual glossary of the flowers and foliage used, see the Flower Glossary on page 136. For alternatives, consult the Substitution List (page 138).

1 Before you start making your arrangement, make sure to carefully condition all your materials (see page 15). Take time to remove any wilted petals and cut the stems with your floral scissors at a 45-degree angle.

2 Begin by putting the hydrangeas into the vase. These should be packed tightly together as they will be acting as our support (a little like floral foam!) and kept close to the rim of the vase. Add in small bunches of Limonium around the hydrangeas to add more body to the base of the soon-to-be arrangement.

3

4

3 Establish your high point with a tall, straight blue delphinium. Add in three more at a slightly lower height. Add another four in the gaps between the previous three, at a slightly lower height. Repeat all the way down until the stems reach the base of the container, in a helter-skelter of delphinium.

4 Now is a good time to add in some more Limonium to break up the severity between the soft, fluffy hydrangeas and the hard, straight lines of the delphinium. At this point you should now have the backbone of your arrangement.

5

5   Fill in the gaps, highlighting the arrangement with white delphinium, working in the same fashion as the previous step. Take care not to break the hydrangeas when adding the delphinium. (Hydrangeas are extremely fragile and a little fussy!) Add one final white delphinium in the center to reestablish a high point and, ta-dah! You've created the Atlantic Ocean, captured in a container.

SWEATER WEATHER

Warmth and texture are plentiful in this arrangement, which is awash with jewel tones and autumnal colors. In addition to stunning dahlias, we will be using deep-toned foliage and branches, the latter being one of my favorite things to use in flower arranging. They add a certain drama and give great height and depth to arrangements. A note here: Buying branches can get quite costly, even at a wholesale price. Whenever you can, try to salvage fallen branches, sticks and twigs. Even if you live in the city like I do, you can usually find fallen branches in parks—just double check with your local authorities first that you're able to take them.

This arrangement is what we call a 180 arrangement, meaning it would be positioned with a wall to its back. In reality, a 180 arrangement needs to look great 75 percent around and "very nice" on the other 25 percent facing the wall (you'll just put fewer flowers here). A great way to think about this is recalling how people may decorate a Christmas tree; in my family, we usually have a side that is facing a corner or a wall with fewer decorations.

Foliage

5 long branches,
for example corylus
1 packet of cotinus

Flowers

1 packet of skimmia
1 packet of orange dahlias
1 packet of deep purple hellebores
1 packet of fuchsia nerine

Supplies

Floral scissors or floral knife
Secateurs
Large, round vase
(I used ceramic, approximately
6 inches [15 cm] in diameter)

For a visual glossary of the flowers and foliage used, see the Flower Glossary on page 136. For alternatives, consult the Substitution List (page 138).

1   Before you start making your arrangement, make sure to carefully condition all your materials (see page 15 on conditioning). Take time to remove any wilted petals and cut the stems with your floral scissors at a 45-degree angle.

2   Start by adding in the branches, using secateurs to cut them if necessary. The branches are the "scaffolding" of this arrangement and will dictate the overall shape and feel of it. Think about how you want your arrangement to look. In mine, I've decided to go higher on one side and lower on another side. These lines will map out where I place the flowers when designing later on.

3   When you're happy with the shape, add in the foliage. In this case, I'm using a beautiful deep-toned cotinus. The foliage should be kept low and just provide body; we don't want it to have any protagonism in the final arrangement.

4   When you're happy that your arrangement has the level of body you want, add in the skimmia. Skimmia is a sort of "bridge" between flowers and foliage. It adds body, but also adds wonderful texture and intrigue. Add in all your stems before moving on to the blooms.

5   Working upward from the foliage, start by adding in the flowers. In flower arranging, larger, heavier flowers should be kept lower down and lighter, daintier flowers higher up. It maintains the balance and makes for a much more aesthetically pleasing result! In this case, our heavier flowers are the dahlias, so place them lower in the arrangement.

6 Next, add in hellebores, varying the height of each stem. Some should be tucked neatly beneath a sprig of foliage and others should start to reach higher up, mirroring the shape and movement of the branches. I think hellebores are an absolutely stunning flower, so I've used quite a lot in my final arrangement.

7 The final step is to add in the nerines. I've chosen a strong color here because I think it really lifts the arrangement and gives it just that little bit of extra oomph it requires. You can, of course, go with a subtler shade for a more muted arrangement. Be mindful of the placement of the nerines—mine grow up and away from the other flowers.

And that's it! You've got autumn in a vase.

MIDNIGHT FAIRIES

I was born and raised in Wales, a land steeped in ancient tradition, legend and myth. Near the town of Briton Ferry, in the south of the country, there is said to be a lake where millennia ago a small town was swallowed up by the dark waters, plunged into the murky depths for all eternity. If, at certain times, you peer into the waters of the lake, it is said that you will find the walls of an impenetrable fairy castle, the home of the Gwragedd Annwn, or Wives of the Lower World. At night, these fairies haunt bodies of water high up in lonely Welsh mountains and act as the vessel of communication between the living and the shadowy underworld of dark fairies.

This is a really simple, yet impactful, vase arrangement using just four ingredients! I've used corylus branches for their movement and swirling, watery forms, but in reality, any branch will work! Hydrangeas add weight and body, while clematis lifts the arrangement and adds a magical touch of lightness—an ode to the shadowy figures of Welsh folklore.

Foliage

10 corylus branches

Flowers

5 brown hydrangeas
1 packet of astrantia
1 packet of clematis

Supplies

Floral scissors or floral knife
Secateurs
A dark vase (12 to 20 inches [30 to 50 cm] in height)

For a visual glossary of the flowers and foliage used, see the Flower Glossary on page 136. For alternatives, consult the Substitution List (page 138).

1   Before you start making your arrangement, make sure to carefully condition all your materials (see page 15). Take time to remove any wilted petals and cut the stems with your floral scissors at a 45-degree angle.

2   First, add your branches to your vase, but reserve one for the end of the arrangement. This is a really important step! The branches are going to be your framework or "scaffolding" for the entire arrangement. Think about your final vase arrangement. How tall do you want to make it? Does it have a high point in the middle like mine, or are you going to make the arrangement peak on the upper left-hand side, for example? The branches provide structure and will be indicative of the final shape of the arrangement.

3   When adding your branches, make sure to keep some at full length and trim others down. This will create height differences and make an arrangement that has more depth and is more attractive to the eye than one in which all the branches are the same length. Don't get hung up on every branch's placement—it's inevitable that they will be moving around as you put more in! As you add the flowers in the next step, the branches will hold still, allowing you to put them into their final positions.

4 Next, add in your hydrangeas. Cut the stems short and pack them in around the rim of the vase. This will be the body of your arrangement. Then add in the astrantia, starting to build your shape. The branches give a great network to follow. Create lines, maps and visual aids for the eyes. Follow the line of one branch upward with a few astrantia and bring them down another. The goal here is to further fill out your arrangement.

5 Following the lines you've made with the branches and astrantia, add in your clematis. Keep the stems as long as possible so that they are almost floating above the rest of the flowers. Clematis do a wonderful job of adding air and movement to any arrangement, so keep this in mind.

6 In arrangements like this, I always save one branch until the very end to mark and accentuate my highest point. Glance at the photo on page 75 for a visual of this. Add that in now, and you're done!

CLEAN LINEN on a SPRING MORNING

White is not strictly a color, rather it is achromatic and sits directly opposite of black, which is the total absorption of color. Much in the same way, the cultural significance of white sits in stark contrast to the brooding and occult of black: Whereas black often symbolizes death, evil and witchcraft, white has long represented light and cleanliness. In floral designing, teaming white with white creates a monochromatic design that is clean, crisp and luxurious—much like newly washed linen on a fresh, bright morning in May. If repeated several times over, this arrangement would make for a stunning wedding table décor. Left alone, this arrangement would be perfect for a dinner with friends in the moment that spring slowly starts to break, melting away the winter chills.

Flowers

1 packet of white carnations
1 packet of white pom pom chrysanthemums
1 packet of white dahlias

Supplies

Floral scissors or floral knife
1 floral foam block
A low, open container or vase (preferably white with
a diameter of 8 to 12 inches [20 to 30 cm])
Floral tape

For a visual glossary of the flowers and foliage used, see the Flower Glossary on page 136. For alternatives, consult the Substitution List (page 138).

1   Begin by roughly cutting the floral foam down to the size of your container. Soak the foam in water, making sure to not push it down. Once fully soaked, place in your container; you may have to cut it down further or push it in with a little force. You want a really snug fit, with no movement of the foam.

2   Make sure it has a snug fit; you don't want to have space around the edges of the container for the floral foam to wobble around. Secure it with floral tape to one edge of the container, and pull over to the other side vertically. Repeat horizontally, so that you make a cross with the floral tape. This will keep the floral foam nice and snug! Floral tape is extremely adhesive, making it a great tool to work with. You can readily find it on Amazon, or at your local florist or plant nursery. Also take a moment to condition your materials (see page 15).

3   Next, map out the shape with carnations. In an asymmetrical arrangement like this one, have some carnations reaching up on one side and others angled toward the floor on the other side. Make sure some carnations are tucked in and others are reaching out to create a visually appealing, three-dimensional arrangement.

4   Continue by adding in the chrysanthemums and dahlia. The chrysanthemums should add body and weight in the central part of the design, while the dahlias should be hovering lightly above the other flowers for added movement and depth.

And that's it! A crisp, clean, super aesthetic design.

CENTER-
PIECES

The easiest way to change a space is to add a floral arrangement. This is a personal opinion, but I think I'm right. Adding flowers to a table can turn a mundane, boring space into one that is brimming with life, soul and flavor. In this chapter, we will be looking at the various ways you can achieve this, creating arrangements that burst with life and vitality and that will instantly cheer up any space.

Once Upon a Midnight Dreary

Once upon a midnight dreary, while I pondered, weak and weary,
Over many a quaint and curious volume of forgotten lore . . .

—Edgar Allen Poe, "The Raven"

"The Raven" is about a person who, desperately traumatized by the death of his love, anxiously tries to escape his reality through reading. Just as he found an exit route in the pages of his novels, we too will find escapism in this brooding and dark table. Transported away from our realities, we will create a table profound and dark, a perfect midnight garden.

Foliage

2 packets of ruscus
1 packet of cotinus

Flowers

1 packet of deep purple hellebores
1 packet of Clooney ranunculus
1 packet of Black Night scabiosa
1 packet of dyed black roses or
Black Baccara roses
1 packet of cosmos

Supplies

Floral scissors or floral knife
1 floral foam block
Black rectangular container
Black water-based spray paint

For a visual glossary of the flowers and foliage used, see the Flower Glossary on page 136. For alternatives, consult the Substitution List (page 138).

1   Begin by roughly cutting the floral foam down to pieces that fit the size and amount of your container. Soak them in water, making sure to not push them down. Once fully soaked, add to your container; you may have to cut them down further or push them in with a little force. You want a really snug fit, with no movement of the foam.

2   After adding the floral foam to the container, place them on the center of the table. You can refresh your knowledge of using floral foam on page 23.

3   After conditioning all your flowers and foliage, spray paint your ruscus leaves. In a well-ventilated area, aim the can directly at the ruscus leaves from 6 to 12 inches (15 to 30 cm) away, and lightly spray each leaf until covered in a layer of black. To brush up on painting natural materials, see page 20.

4   Add in the foliage, making sure to cover the floral foam as best you can. I've cut the cotinus to 4 to 6 inches (10 to 15 cm).

6B

6C

5   When designing centerpieces with floral foam, it is imperative to think about how flowers grow in the wild, even if there is nothing "natural" about the design in question (as is the case of our midnight garden). Flowers usually grow together in little groups, with the occasional odd one out shooting off somewhere else. Close your eyes for a moment and think about a garden in full bloom: Taller, structural flowers rise from the hedgerow; robust, heavier flowers give body and depth to the flower bed; and the daintiest, most elegant little flowers will oftentimes dance above their flower friends below.

6   Bearing the previous point in mind, start creating your midnight garden. It helps me to start first with the taller flowers (here, the hellebores) to establish the highest points of my design, arranging them close together but varying the height of each stem slightly. I'll then add in the flowers that will make up the body of the arrangement (in this case, ranunculus, scabiosa and roses), and finally, the little cosmos hovering above the rest.

7   Finally, take a moment to play around with height and depth—pull some stems out a little and push others in. Try to avoid taking stems out completely and reinserting them back in again, as this will over-perforate the floral foam and cause it to disintegrate.

ARCTIC BREEZE

This arrangement is a simple yet visually impactful tablescape. We're going to be using several different vases of varying sizes and creating a table runner full of texture and movement while using very few flowers. Bud vases are a great, inexpensive option for creating an impactful tablescape. They're also incredibly simple to arrange with and don't require a great deal of creativity. Each vase is typically only a couple of centimeters wide at the top and will fit a couple of stems.

Instead of arranging each vase individually, we will arrange by flower. That's to say, we will start by setting the table and laying out the vases. Then, we'll add one flower type at a time until all our flowers have been used up.

For arrangements like this one, it's important not to get weighed down by the small details and overanalyze every single vase. After all, some vases may only contain two or three stems. Rather, in table runners like this we're going for the overall effect. In this case, a table that transports us to the far north as we gaze out over the freezing arctic glaciers.

Flowers

1 packet of white delphiniums
1 packet of white lisianthus
1 packet of white dahlias
1 packet of white spray roses

Supplies

Floral scissors or floral knife
4 to 5 white ceramic bud vases of varying heights (or any small vases)

For a visual glossary of the flowers and foliage used, see the Flower Glossary on page 136. For alternatives, consult the Substitution List (page 138).

1 Begin by choosing your vases. Your choice of vase is really important and will set the mood for the whole event! A clear glass bud vase will feel open and airy, while a ceramic one will lend a more grounded and heavier element to your design. You can also choose different heights, similar to what I've done here.

2 Next, fill up your vases with water—aim to fill one-third to one-half full. Then, arrange your empty vases on the table. Have taller vases in between place settings and shorter ones directly in front of plates—that way, you will always be able to see the person sitting in front of you. Whenever possible, I always set out my vases before arranging as it's much easier to visualize. Take this time to condition your flowers (see more on conditioning on page 15).

3

4A

4B

3   Next, add your flowers! I usually do it by flower type. I'll start by adding in all the delphiniums, cutting the stems at different heights to create visual variation and interest.

4   Then, I'll go through and add the lisianthus and dahlias before finishing off with a few spray roses. In some vases, I'll add four or five stems, and in others, just one or two. Considering the whole design is more important than the individual in arrangements like this one.

And that's it! You have an incredibly simple, arctic-inspired table arrangement.

LIFE THRIVES AT THE EQUATOR

This arrangement is tall, impactful, bordering on extra and . . . extremely easy to create! The first time I made this arrangement was for a wedding. It was a tropical-themed event, and four of the eight tables needed something big and impactful. We landed on palm leaves arranged on flower pedestals. And that's essentially what this arrangement is! A collection of different tropical greenery, arranged to look like a tree in the rainforest. Flower pedestals, or floral/plant stands, are readily available on Amazon. If you can't find them, you can use anything else that is tall and to which floral foam can be attached—a tall candelabra without candles would work well here.

Foliage

2 packets of palm leaves (30 to 40 inches [80 to 100 cm] tall)
1 packet of coconut leaves
1 packet of foxtail fern
1 packet of monstera leaves
2 packets of ruscus

Supplies

Floral scissors or floral knife
4 floral foam blocks
Zip ties
A tall plant pedestal/stand (30 to 40 inches [80 to 100 cm] tall)
Leaf shine (optional)

For a visual glossary of the flowers and foliage used, see the Flower Glossary on page 136. For alternatives, consult the Substitution List (page 138).

1   Start by placing four blocks of presoaked, standard-sized floral foam on top of the plant stand. For a refresher on working with floral foam, see page 23. Secure the blocks carefully with zip ties.

2   Instead of covering the mechanics as you usually would, start by adding in the long palm leaves. It's a good idea to buy a couple of different lengths, even if you are going to trim down the leaves. The final arrangement is going to look like a tree. When adding in the palm leaves, keep this shape at the front of your mind. Place one leaf shooting directly upward, another out to the side, and another facing downward, just like a palm tree. Remember, all the material needs to look as though it is radiating out of the same central spot, buried somewhere deep inside the floral foam. Bearing this in mind, have all leaves radiating out from this central nucleus.

3 Add in the coconut leaves. These are much shorter than the palm leaves and should be focused around the center of the arrangement. Intersperse the arrangement with larger, textural monstera leaves and foxtail ferns, following the lines you just created with the palm leaves.

4 Next, cover the mechanisms, or rather, the floral foam atop the stand/podium. Cut your ruscus (which is what I've used here, but you can use whichever type of foliage you prefer) to 4 to 6 inches (10 to 15 cm) and add the stems into the arrangement, keeping close to the base. A note here on cutting ruscus (or any foliage): 1 stem of ruscus will usually yield two or three good-sized pieces. To have fewer visible cuts on your foliage stems, always cut just above a leaf and at a 45-degree angle. This will make the hard edge a lot less visible than if you cut a stem horizontally between leaves. If you'd like, add leaf shine to the larger leaves in your piece for an added pop.

AUTUMN SUNSET

"Fall, leaves, fall; die, flowers, away;
Lengthen night and shorten day;
Every leaf speaks bliss to me;
Fluttering from the Autumn tree,"

—Emily Brontë, "Fall, Leaves, Fall"

This imagery, of falling leaves, shortening days, the first frosty bite of winter and lengthy mid-afternoon sunsets will form the inspiration for the following centerpiece. I've decided to use pumpkins, with floral foam inside, as my vessel of choice. I just think they look so good and add an extra touch of fall to the table! You could also use a low, open container. Now, let's go! An arrangement brimming with the last vibrant push of autumn as she delivers herself into winter.

Foliage

1 packet of magnolia branches
2 packets of cotinus

Supplies

Floral scissors or floral knife
3 or 4 pumpkins
1–2 floral foam blocks
Large knife

Flowers

2 packets of white dahlias
1 packet of brown trachelium
1 packet of brown lisianthus
1 packet of burgundy scabiosa
1 packet of dark red roses
1 packet of dried grasses,
for example pampas grass
1 packet of dried scabiosa pods

For a visual glossary of the flowers and foliage used, see the Flower Glossary on page 136. For alternatives, consult the Substitution List (page 138).

1   We're going to start by turning a pumpkin into a vase (no magic involved, I promise). The first step is to hollow out the pumpkin, as if you were making a jack-o'-lantern. Cut the top off, scoop out all the seeds and scrape all those dangly bits off the edges. Then cut your floral foam to fit into the pumpkin and presoak (you can read more about working with floral foam on page 23). Exerting a little pressure from above, push the foam down into the pumpkin so that it fits nice and snug inside. And that's it! A usable pumpkin vase. Flowers should stay fresh for 3 to 5 days inside the pumpkins.

2   Map out your tablescape. I've cut smaller blocks of floral foam to go in between the pumpkins, and I've saved the "lids" (or pumpkin tops) to add some more interest to the table. These aspects are optional. Take this time to condition your flowers and foliage (read more on conditioning on page 15).

3   Add the foliage into the floral foam. I'm using magnolia branches for their brown-toned leaves and beautiful deep purple cotinus, but any foliage will work here. The aim here is to conceal all the floral foam from sight but leave enough space for our flowers. I recommend covering 60 to 70 percent of the foam.

4   Establish the high points and overall shape of the arrangement with the dahlias. Remember that in nature, flowers never grow in solitude, rather they grow in patches together. Grouping the dahlias together, try to evoke a bed of flowers growing happily together. It will be much more aesthetically pleasing than flowers spaced randomly throughout.

5   Next, add the trachelium and lisianthus, but much lower down than the dahlias. These are textural elements and shouldn't have any starring role by the time we're done.

6   Create a bridge between the tall dahlias and lisianthus by adding in scabiosa and roses. As the scabiosa is a daintier, lighter flower, it makes sense to add them high above the lisianthus, almost as if they were dancing above the other blooms, and the red roses slightly lower down given their physical and visual weight.

7   Finish up by emphasizing any high points or points of interest with pampas grass. As it is a tall, straight line, the eye will first be drawn to these points before working its way down the arrangement. As a final touch, add in dried scabiosa pods high above the rest of the arrangement, a nod to the garden's final push before the cold hand of winter takes hold.

EXTRAVAGANT
ELEMENTS

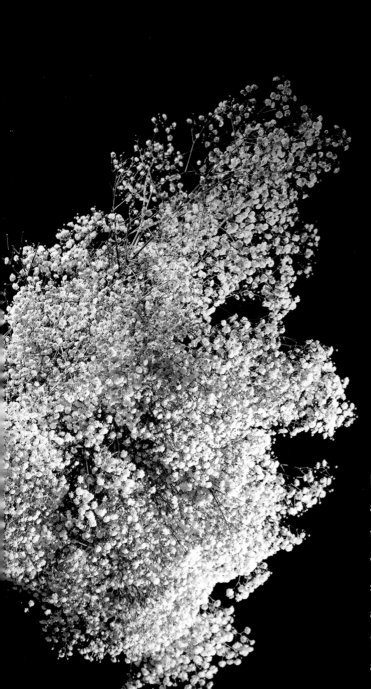

In this chapter, we're going to have fun. Using all the skills and techniques you've learned thus far, you're going to get deeply creative with flowers, transitioning from a place of seeing a flower as a flower to seeing a flower as an artistic medium. This is crucial in your floral journey. When you start to see a flower as a painter would see their paints, the sky is the limit.

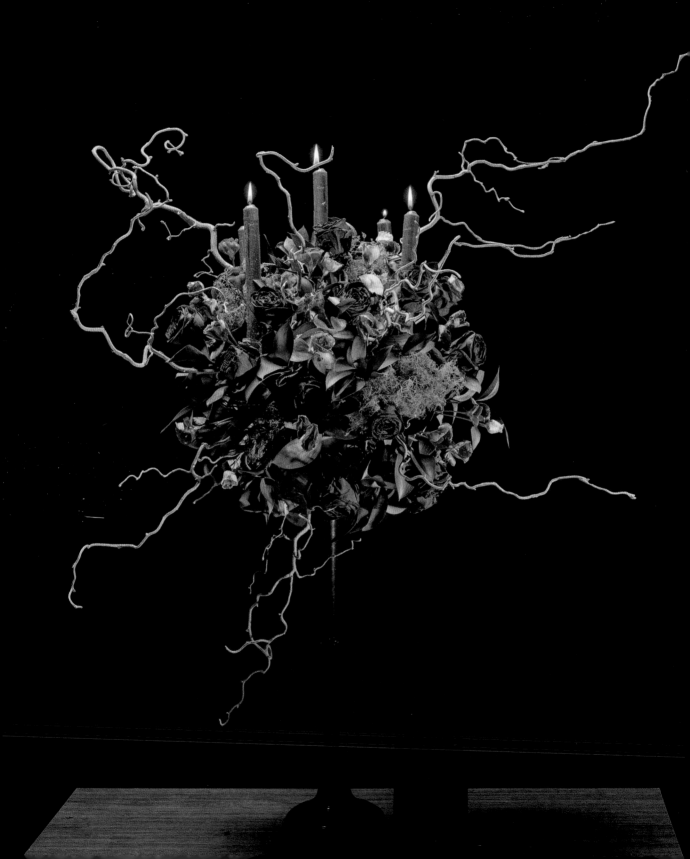

REQUIEM

If you were music, I would listen to you ceaselessly,
And my low spirits would brighten up.

—Anna Akhmatova, "Requiem"

"Requiem" is a poem written against the backdrop of the Great Purge. It is a tale of loss and despair, yet also hope and love. It is these concepts that I wanted to thread through the candelabra we will be making together. It is a black arrangement, dark and brooding, but it is lit up with candles to brighten up a table. Candelabras are surprisingly easy to come by: A quick search on Amazon will show you hundreds of options! I'd recommend getting one around 30 inches (80 cm) tall. Any smaller and you risk not being able to see those sitting opposite you (maybe that would work well for certain family dinners though!) and any taller would risk throwing off the proportions of the table setting.

Foliage

4 bunches of ruscus
1 packet of cotinus
5 to 6 corylus branches

Supplies

Floral scissors or floral knife
Black water-based spray paint
30-inch (80-cm) candelabra
2 blocks of floral foam
Black candles

Flowers

10 Black Pearl lisianthus stems
12 dyed rose stems

For a visual glossary of the flowers and foliage used, see the Flower Glossary on page 136. For alternatives, consult the Substitution List (page 138).

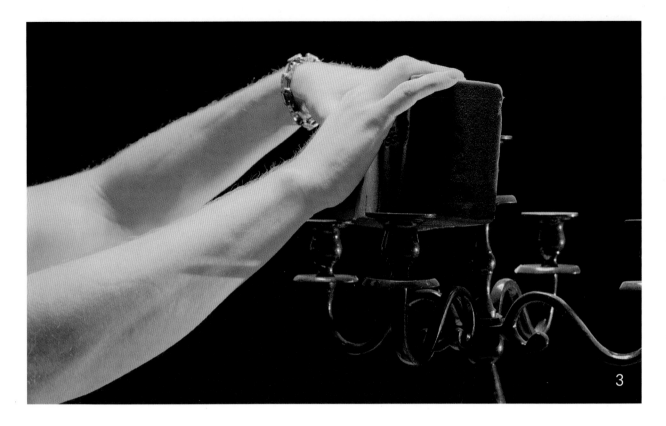

3

1 Before you begin, there is a bit of prep work to be done! After you have conditioned all your flowers (to read more on conditioning, see page 15), start by painting your ruscus. In a well-ventilated area (or outside), hold your spray paint can 6 to 12 inches (15 to 30 cm) away from the ruscus leaves and cover in an even layer of black. To brush up on how to spray paint natural materials, see page 20.

2 Once the ruscus is fully dry (usually 1 to 2 hours, depending on climate), cut it into 6-inch (15-cm) pieces. One stem of ruscus will usually yield two to three good-sized pieces. To have fewer visible cuts on your foliage stems, always cut just above a leaf and at a 45-degree angle. This will make the hard edge a lot less visible than if you cut a stem horizontally between leaves.

3 Begin by presoaking your floral foam (to learn more about how to soak floral foam, see page 23), and press the blocks down firmly between the candelabra arms. Make sure the top of the block doesn't rise too much above the candleholder. It's normal for a lot of water to come out as you exert pressure on the floral foam from above, so make sure to have a towel at hand.

4 The first step is to insert the candles and create a shape using the precut ruscus. The final shape of the finished candelabra is going to be round, so when inserting the foliage, bear this in mind. For example, on the top, the foliage is going to be angled directly upward, and on the bottom, directly downward. On the upper corner, the ruscus is going to be angled up and outward at the same angle as the corner, and on the bottom corner, down and away, again, at the same angle. I always start by mapping out the final shape of the candelabra, before filling it in with the rest of the foliage. Add in the cotinus after.

6

5   How do you know if you've added enough foliage, or if you need to add some more? Basically, all the mechanisms (i.e., floral foam) should be concealed from the eye, but there should still be enough space to add in your flowers. Let's say, 60 to 70 percent covered by foliage.

6   When you're happy with the final shape of your candelabra, it's time to add in your flowers. There's no rhyme or reason here, but there are a couple of things to bear in mind. First, a candelabra has candles (i.e., open flames!). I always add in my candles before anything else so that I never go higher than them with flowers or go too close and create a fire hazard. Always keep an eye on your candles, as you don't want the arrangement to go up in flames. Second, group your flowers in a way that looks realistic. In the wild, flowers never grow alone, so think about this when designing. Group several lisianthus around the base of one candle, having some reaching out while others are tucked in. Group some roses together on the lower edge to look like a fantasy rose bush.

7   The final stage is to add in branches. I've chosen corylus for their movement, but any branch, provided it isn't dead-straight, will work just fine. Evenly space out the branches throughout your arrangement to create line and form.

8   Light the candles and watch how your low spirits brighten up.

PASTEL CLOUDS

Despite being so striking, baby's breath clouds are surprisingly easy to make. As they are lightweight and don't require watering, installation is also a breeze. You can also make these fluffy, ethereal clouds as big or as small as you want. And this same technique can be used to make garlands, wreaths or even centerpieces. If you don't have access to baby's breath you can easily swap it out for Limonium, for example.

I've chosen to do this project in pastel blue tones, but you can choose any color you want. Remember to get several cans of spray paint in varying tones and hues for maximum impact. In the introductory chapters, you'll have noticed that I wrote of the importance of using a water-based spray paint when painting natural materials, but this is not the case for baby's breath! Any spray paint will work just fine. For this project, a little light construction work may be needed! Make sure you have all the supplies and a friend at hand to help!

Flowers
3 to 4 packets of baby's breath

Supplies
Floral scissors
Various shades of blue spray paint
Chicken wire
Wire cutters
Cable ties
A ladder
Wall/ceiling hooks (if necessary)
Strong nylon thread
Power drill (if necessary)

For a visual glossary of the flowers and foliage used, see the Flower Glossary on page 136. For alternatives, consult the Substitution List (page 138).

1   Before we start, you're going to want to spray paint your baby's breath. As I explained, I think a variety of shades works better than one solid color, but taste and aesthetic are decidedly subjective . . . so do what works best for you! In a well-ventilated area, spray paint your baby's breath. Aim the can directly at the leaves from about 12 inches (30 cm) away, and lightly spray in an even layer of paint. To brush up on painting natural materials, see page 20. Set aside and leave to dry. Besides the painting, this project requires no extra flower conditioning!

2   Building a strong, secure base is perhaps the most important step in this whole project! You don't want to make a fabulous floral cloud, only for it to collapse seconds later. Start by making a long "sausage" of chicken wire, then double it back over on itself. The initial sausage should be around three times the length of the desired size for the floral cloud. Once doubled, scrunch the chicken wire in on itself to create folds and grooves; these will later serve as support for the stems so they have something to grip on to. Secure the loose ends with cable ties.

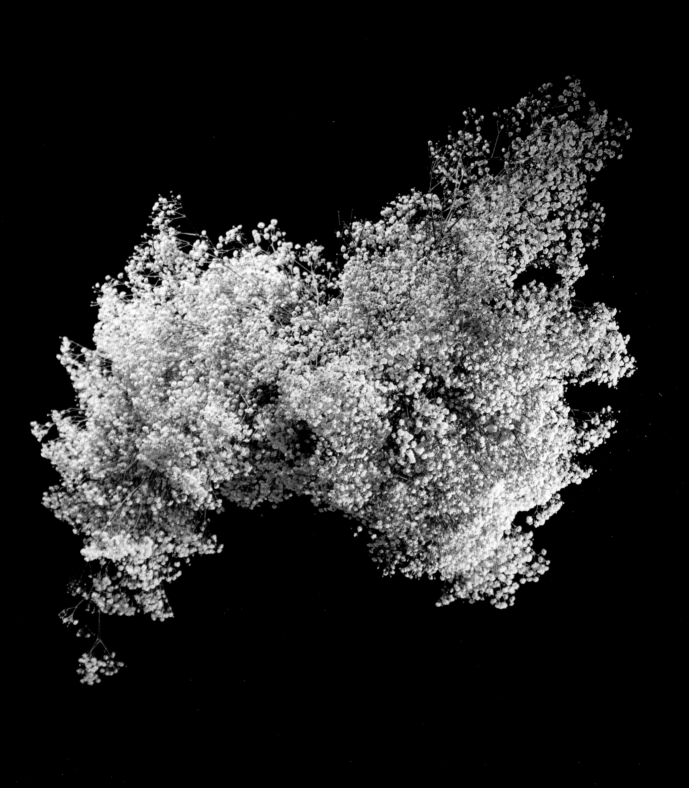

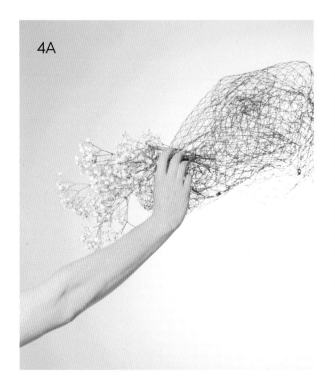

4A

4B

4C

3   Using hooks, if necessary, attach your chicken wire to the ceiling by means of a strong nylon thread (fishing line works great here!). Once suspended, you won't be able to move the installation, so make sure you're happy with its final hanging position! It's a good idea to suspend it in four or five places. This spreads the weight and stops the installation from moving around so much. You may need a ladder and power drill for this step.

4   Begin by inserting small bunches of baby's breath into the suspended chicken wire, making sure to gradate the colors as per your desired design.

5

5 And that's kind of it! Continue adding small bunches of baby's breath until the installation has reached your desired shape, size and fullness. We did various arrangements for maximum impact for the book, but one is also perfect.

HERA

A wedding arch acts as the backdrop to your wedding ceremony. You can also have it at the entryway to the venue, setting the mood and feel for the day. If you want, you can also use it to take photos with. There's just one problem—archways can add hundreds, if not thousands, of dollars to your wedding bill. In light of this, many soon-to-be-weds are choosing to DIY their wedding florals. With a little creativity, a bit of help and some flowers, creating your dream wedding becomes both accessible and affordable. Keep in mind, though, that this arch is flower-heavy, so it's still costly. If you need to tighten your budget a little, use more greenery and fewer flowers. It is an inexpensive way to create a lot of body and cover your archway and floral foam.

Hera, the Greek goddess of fertility, marriage and childbirth lends her name to this project in a nod toward her presiding over union and matrimony.

Flowers

5 packets of white carnations
10 packets of white chrysanthemums
10 packets of white dahlias
10 packets of white spray roses
8 packets of white roses
10 packets of white delphinium

Supplies

Floral scissors or floral knife
A freestanding wedding arch (you can get these on Amazon or at your local garden center)
Heavy rocks or sandbags
6 floral foam bricks
10 trays floral foam blocks or floral foam garlands
Cable ties
Wire

For a visual glossary of the flowers and foliage used, see the Flower Glossary on page 136. For alternatives, consult the Substitution List (page 138).

1   We're going to start with the mechanisms. Make sure you're happy with where your arch is (it's a nightmare to move after creating—trust me!), and if necessary, add extra weight to the base with heavy rocks. Place three floral foam bricks at the base of the arch—one on the left, one in front of the base, and one to the right of the base. You might want to put a plastic covering on the floor underneath the floral foam to protect it from water spills. Repeat on the other side.

2   Next, we're going to add floral foam "cages". The cage is essentially the same as normal floral foam, the only difference being that it is encased in a thin plastic cage, which helps to attach it to a structure. Holding the cage vertically against the arch, cable-tie it on in several places. I cable-tied mine at the top, the bottom and on both sides. More is more here! You don't want your flowers falling down halfway through the ceremony. This step can be a little fiddly, and four hands are better than two. Make sure to "taper" your floral foam up—the base of the arch should be denser than the top. This will give it a much more natural feel and add stability to the installation!

3   Cable-tie more floral foam cages all the way around the arch, leaving 6 to 8 inches (15 to 20 cm) of space between each block. Make sure each block is secured in at least ten different points. Take this time to condition your flowers (read more on conditioning on page 15).

4

4   Begin with the "filler" flowers. These will be cheaper blooms that cover a lot of surface area. Here, I've chosen carnations and chrysanthemums. When inserting your flowers, make sure that they are all facing upward and outward, sitting at a 30- to 45-degree angle. When you face your flowers up, they look alive and happy; when they're peering toward the ground, they look dead, dull and drab.

5

5 Concentrate your last remaining filler flowers around the base of the arrangement, where it should be the fullest. Don't worry if you can still see the floral foam around the arch—we will cover this with more flowers later.

6A

6B

7

6   Next, add in the dahlias. Again, angled up-ward, making sure they sit higher than the carnations and chrysanthemums to start introducing height, depth and movement to an otherwise static arch. Once complete, add in the spray roses and regular roses. Rather than spacing the roses out evenly, try clumping them together to form thickets of roses around the base and sides of the arch. Some roses should be reaching up high and others tucked away timidly. This will make for a much more natural arch. Repeat with the roses and focus this time on covering all the mechanisms that you can still see.

7   Insert the longer stemmed delphinium into the base, arranging in clusters. I've also intro-duced delphiniums higher up to add move-ment and texture to the arch. And that's it! An ode to Hera, the goddess of marriage.

COOL at YULE

Christmas is one of my favorite times of the year. Actually, all holidays are. While I love decorating, I never really associate Christmas with being a particularly "floral" holiday. We have trees, wreaths, garlands, etc., but we never really see fresh arrangements! At least not in my house, anyway. Wanting to change that, I'm going to show you how to make a festive centerpiece to add life and vitality to the most wonderful time of the year.

I've made and photographed this "wreath" lying flat to hold a candle inside. While it is envisaged to be a centerpiece, there is nothing stopping you from hanging this design vertically on your door. Just remember that if using fresh flowers, it will be an ephemeral, fleeting moment of yuletide beauty, rather than a typical wreath that lasts the entire festive period.

Foliage

2 packets of ruscus, or any hardy greenery

Flowers

5 branches of cotton
1 packet of dried lunaria (you can find dried flowers at most major stores including Target, but if not, Amazon has a great selection)
2 packets of white dahlias

Supplies

Floral scissors or floral knife
8- to 10-inch (20- to 25-cm) floral foam wreath (these are available online from most stores including Joann Fabrics and Hobby Lobby or on Amazon)
Gold spray paint
Candle

For a visual glossary of the flowers and foliage used, see the Flower Glossary on page 136. For alternatives, consult the Substitution List (page 138).

1   Start by soaking your floral foam wreath. As these have a hardy plastic backing, it's unlikely that it will sink to the bottom of your container. When it stops bubbling, you can be confident that it is properly soaked. While you wait for the floral foam to soak, paint your ruscus in a light spray of gold spray paint so that the green still shows through. In a well-ventilated area, aim the can directly at the leaves from 6 to 12 inches (15 to 30 cm) away, and lightly spray each leaf until covered in a light layer of gold. Spray paint a few sprigs all gold. To brush up on painting natural materials, see page 20. Set aside to dry. I've chosen to paint about 70 percent of my greenery—it just gives it a much more natural feel!

2   Once your greenery is dry to the touch (depending on the brand of spray paint, 30 minutes to 1 hour), cut them into short, 6- to 8-inch (15- to 20-cm) pieces. Each stem of greenery usually yields three or four usable pieces. Remember to cut greenery just above a leaf at a 45-degree angle—that way, your cut mark will be a lot less visible.

3   Start to cover the floral wreath with ruscus. Working clockwise, make sure that all greenery is going in the same direction, and that you cover both the top and the sides.

4 Cut the cotton off the cotton branches, leaving small pieces of branch to insert into the foam, and space the cotton pieces out evenly around the wreath.

5 Add in the lunaria, creating height and movement. Remember to continue working clockwise, grouping your dried materials in an aesthetically pleasing way.

6   Finally, add in the dahlias. Try cutting some stems short and tucking them away near the foliage and leave others longer—this will create a much more dynamic wreath!

7   Finally, add in your candle to the center of the arrangement for a final Christmassy touch! To see a visual of this, peek at the photo on page 121. Keep an eye on your candle, as you don't want the arrangement to go up in flames.

TELL ME HOW MEN KISS YOU

Tablescaping has become a huge trend in recent years. I, for one, enjoy scrolling through endless boards of photos on Pinterest in an evening, admiring the creativity and talent of people worlds over, united in their shared love for decorating tables. This floral candelabra is perfect for an intimate dinner. Sometimes, candelabra arrangements can feel very big and imposing, so I've gone for soft pastels to keep the table light and airy. I've chosen a gold candelabra and decided to use soft cream candles to maintain the ethereal, light feeling inherent to the pastel-toned florals.

Foliage

1 packet of ruscus

Flowers

1 packet of pink carnations
1 packet of pink lisianthus
1 packet of pink spray roses
1 packet of white roses
1 packet of light pink garden roses
1 packet of white delphinium

Supplies

Floral scissors or floral knife
Gold spray paint
1 floral foam block
12- to 16-inch (30- to 40-cm)
candelabra
Candles

For a visual glossary of the flowers and foliage used, see the Flower Glossary on page 136. For alternatives, consult the Substitution List (page 138).

3

1   Soak your floral foam (to learn more about
    how to soak floral foam, see page 23). Once
    it's done soaking, press the block down
    firmly between the candelabra arms. Make
    sure the top of the block doesn't rise too
    much above the candleholder. It's normal
    for a lot of water to come out as you exert
    pressure on the floral foam from above, so
    make sure to have a towel at hand.

2   In a well-ventilated area, spray paint your
    ruscus leaves. Aim the can directly at the
    leaves from 6 to 12 inches (15 to 30 cm)
    away, and lightly spray each leaf until
    covered in a layer of gold. To brush up on
    painting natural materials, see page 20. Set
    aside and leave to dry.

3   Once the ruscus is dry to the touch (usu-
    ally an hour or less, depending on which
    brand of paint you use), cut the ruscus into
    6- to 8-inch (15- to 20-cm) pieces. Add the
    candles to the candelabra and begin insert-
    ing the foliage into the floral foam.

5A

5B

4   The final shape of the finished candelabra is going to be round, so when inserting the foliage, bear this in mind. For example, on the upper corner, the ruscus is going to be angled up and outward at the same angle as the corner, and on the bottom corner, down and away, again, at the same angle. I always start by mapping out the final shape of the candelabra, before filling it in with the rest of the foliage.

5   Next, we're going to use our cheapest flowers to cover the mechanisms (i.e., the floral foam). In this case, the flower of choice is the carnation! Carnations tend to get a bit of a bad rep, which is completely unjustified. They're really affordable filler flowers that come in plenty of different tones and shades, and they really don't deserve the reputation they've quite unfortunately gained. Using the carnations as a filler, start to conceal the floral foam from sight. Once most of the floral foam is covered, add in the lisianthus and the smaller spray roses.

6A

6B

6   Next, add in the heavier flowers, making sure to keep them close to the base of the arrangement. In this case, it's the white roses and garden roses. Think about the end goal. How do you want the candelabra to look? Do you want to create something symmetrical, or would you like a more wild-looking candelabra, with blooms shooting out everywhere? Add the roses accordingly, either neat and symmetrical, or wild and free. You don't need many here. With such spectacular blooms like garden roses, less is definitely more. Try grouping some together at different heights—it'll make for a much more natural-looking arrangement.

7 Finish by adding in the delphinium. I've cut off the top 6 to 8 inches (15 to 20 cm) of the blooms (the most delicate part) to add movement to the arrangement, not to add a strong line. The delphinium should be floating above the rest of the arrangement. Some should come up and out, others should reach down and away to create dimension and visual interest.

8 Finally, light up the candles for an incredible night ahead. Make sure to always keep an eye on your candles, as you don't want the arrangement to go up in flames.

OF THINGS WILD

There is no better time to visit the UK than June. Long days and short nights, the countryside is in full bloom. The balmy nights bring with them the scent of honeysuckle, roses and countryside. The latter I can't explain, but I'm sure you know how it smells. It is a grounding smell. Wet earth, rain, growth. I love to walk for hours with my mum through these verdant landscapes, breathing, rooting and connecting both with myself and the world that surrounds me. I've lived for many years abroad, but nothing comes close to a beautiful summer night in the UK.

This piece is an ode to the British countryside and would be perfect for a wedding, or even a dinner. It's quick and easy to assemble and, due to the fact that we're using hardy greenery, lasts for a really long time. It could be used on top of a mantelpiece, on a podium, or even as a table centerpiece.

Foliage

1 packet of viburnum laurustinus
1 packet of ruscus
1 packet of magnolia
1 packet of camelia
1 packet of Myers asparagus fern
1 packet of green Thlaspi

Supplies

Floral scissors or floral knife
1 floral foam block

For a visual glossary of the flowers and foliage used, see the Flower Glossary on page 136. For alternatives, consult the Substitution List (page 138).

1   Presoak the floral foam block, and place in the middle of the table or within your container (for a refresher on using floral foam, see page 23).

2   With your longest branches—I've used the viburnum laurustinus—begin by mapping out the shape. I wanted to go with a really natural, relaxed feel, so I've taken one branch up to the left and another down to the right. Even with just two branches inserted, the shape is clear. Cutting the branches at shorter lengths, fill out the ends. Make sure to leave two or three longer branches for the end.

3   Using shorter-leaved greenery, cover your mechanism. Here, I've gone with ruscus, magnolia and camelia. Any greenery will work here, but make sure you find differences in color and texture. If all your greenery is the same shade of green, you'll create an overwhelmingly one-dimensional arrangement.

4   Continue adding body and shape to the mantel with different greenery. I'm adding in the wonderfully textural fern and Thlaspi, grouping them together as I go along the mantelpiece to create pockets of color and intrigue.

5   Finally, add in the longest branches you initially put to one side. Adding them at the ends of the arrangement will accentuate your original lines and breathe life and dimension into the mantelpiece. Take a peek at the photo on page 131 for a visual on this.

That's it! The English countryside atop a fire.

TiME to BLOSSOM

In this chapter, you'll find an exhaustive list of alternatives for the blooms used in this book and a visual flower glossary to help you better identify different varieties. We're also going to talk about the next steps in your floral journey—where you can go, what you can do and how you can deepen your knowledge and love of all things floral.

Flower Glossary

Allium

Astilbe

Astrantia

Baby's breath

Black Baccara roses

Calla lilies

Carnations

Clematis

Coconut leaves

Corylus

Cotinus

Cosmos

Dahlias

Delphinium

Dianthus

Foxtail

Hellebores

Hydrangeas

Hypericum

Limonium

Lisianthus

Nerine

Palm leaf

Queen Anne's lace

Roses

Ruscus

Safflower

Salix

Scabiosa pods

Skimmia

Snowberries

Spray roses

Trachelium

Veronica

Viburnums

Substitution List

Alstroemeria: Spray rose, Spider lily, Tiger lily, Merrybells, Martagon lily, Nerine

Astilbe: Veronica, Limonium, Amaranthus

Astrantia: Bouvardia, Brunia, Spray rose, Spray carnation, Sweet pea

Baby's Breath: Limonium, Statice, Wax flower, Heather, Queen Anne's lace, Daucus, Solidago, Mimosa

Calla Lily: Trumpet lily, Tuberose

Carnation: Spray rose, Zinnia, Alstroemeria, Chrysanthemum

Chrysanthemum: Carnation, Spray rose, Zinnia, Alstroemeria

Clematis: Cosmos, Butterfly Ranunculus, Freesia, Japanese anemone

Corylus: Salix, Pussy willow, Any branches

Cosmos: Butterfly Ranunculus, Clematis, Japanese anemone

Cotinus: Photinia, Viburnum, Physocarpus Diabolo, Leucadendron 'Sunset Safari'

Dahlia: Zinnia, Pom Pom Gerbera

Delphinium: Foxglove (digitalis), Stock (wallflower), Gladiolus, Hollyhock, Baptisia, Larkspur, Tuberose, Bells of Ireland, Eremurus

Eryngium (thistle): Echinops, Allium

Freesia: Tuberose

Gladiolus: Foxglove (digitalis), Stock (wallflower), Delphinium, Hollyhock, Baptisia, Larkspur, Tuberose, Bells of Ireland, Eremurus

Helleborus: Anemone, Ranunculus, Poppy

Hydrangea: Carnations, Sedum, Queen Anne's lace

Hypericum: Viburnum

Larkspur: Foxglove (digitalis), Stock (wallflower), Gladiolus, Hollyhock, Baptisia, Delphinium, Tuberose, Bells of Ireland, Eremurus

Leucadendron: Photinia, Pysocarpus Diabolo, Cotinus

Limonium: Baby's breath, Wax flower, Statice, Heather, Queen Anne's lace, Daucus, Solidago, Mimosa

Lisianthus: Spray rose, Ranunculus

Miscanthus: Feather grass, Stypha

Nigella: Ranunculus, Cornflower, Scabiosa

Peony: Garden rose, Lisianthus, Ranunculus

Photinia: Cotinus, Painted ruscus, Acer

Poppy: Helleborus, Ranunculus, Anemone

Ranunculus: Spray rose, Helleborus, Lisianthus

Rose: Double tulip, Lisianthus, Ranunculus, Peony

Ruscus: Eucalyptus, Italian ruscus, Camelia. In reality, any greenery can substitute ruscus

Salix: Corylus, Pussy willow, Any branches

Scabiosa: Ranunculus, Dahlia, Cornflower, Nigella, Strawflower

Scabiosa Pod: Poppy pod, Lunaria seed pod, Nigella seed pod

Spray Rose: Lisianthus, Spray carnations, Ranunculus

Sweet Pea: Butterfly Ranunculus, Astrantia, Fritillaria, Forget-Me-Nots

Veronica: Astilbe

Your Floral Journey

What's next? That depends on you, on your hopes and dreams, goals and objectives. If you're a hobby florist and want to learn more about flowers, the internet is your best friend. We are truly blessed to have thousands, if not millions, of hours of free content available to consume across various social media platforms. Get inspired on Pinterest and Instagram or watch more in-depth videos on YouTube. Start to put together groups of images of arrangements you like, and more important, ask yourself why you like them. Analyze the images: What flowers has the creator used? Which techniques went in to creating the composition? Start experimenting with flowers, with color, with texture, and start building up your own personal style. Practice, practice, practice. Forge a deeper bond with natural materials. Gift flower arrangements that you make to friends and family, romanticize your life and have fresh flowers at home, throw a dinner party and be that person who does extra and decorates the entire table as if it were a wedding. And most important, have fun.

If you're thinking about taking floral design more seriously, I'm so happy for you! This is going to be one of the best decisions you ever make, and you're going to be absolutely amazing. Consider signing up for a course, either on-line or in person: Many florists in your area will offer in-person courses, which are a great way to meet like-minded people and have a fun day. There are plenty of schools that offer longer, more in-depth floral design courses too. I also have an online course (acfloralstudio.teachable.com) where I go over the concepts mentioned in this book in more detail and walk you through new, fresh designs.

Consider, too, doing an apprenticeship or helping out at your local florist, or applying for a floral job. As with any creative pursuit, practice makes perfect and the more you create, the better and more proficient you will become. But I just have this feeling that you're going to be incredible.

ACKNOWLEDGMENTS

Thank you to Franny, my editor at Page Street Publishing, for believing in me from the get-go. It is safe to say that this incredible project would never have happened without you. Thank you to Gonçalo, without whose steadfast support and unconditional love I would never have become a florist in the first place. Thank you to Emma, for keeping me grounded and for always bringing me back to my essence when I most need it. To Mum, for bringing me onto this earthly plane and for being the best cheerleader and friend I could wish for. To Emily for unconditional love. To Ricardo for hours of dedication, love and support, without which I wouldn't be the florist I am today. To all my friends for consistently supporting me when I have been tired, stressed and crabby throughout my floral journey and for continually being understanding and loving. To the higher power who I know guides everything in life.

This book would not be what it is without the incredible photography skills of Rafa, who I thank from the bottom of my heart for making visual masterpieces time after time. I'm so grateful to Lianne and Gerben at Hoek for providing some of the flowers and making this project possible. Heartfelt thanks to Jos and Jorge for their extraordinary generosity and providing us with an incredible space where this project could blossom. My eternal gratitude goes out to all my incredible followers on social media, many of whom have been with me right from the beginning, for believing in me, for interacting with my content, for sending me positive messages of encouragement and cheering me up with countless comments of love. And finally, I'd like to thank Queenie, who I know is constantly holding my hand from the other side.

ABOUT the AUTHOR and PHOTOGRAPHER

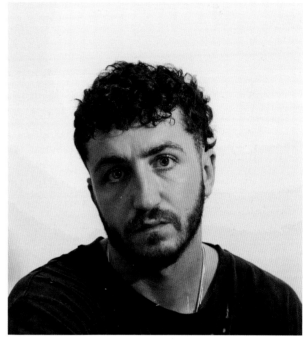

Alexander Campbell is a British florist and content creator currently based in Madrid. He is interested in ephemeral, fleeting moments of beauty and the crossroads at which nature becomes art, manipulated by the hands of another. A vested interest in poetry, literature, pop culture and visual art guide Alex in his pursuit of the transcendence of natural materials, with the objective of democratizing floral design and creating a wider appreciation of flowers. Alexander started his company AC Floral Studio during the pandemic in 2020 and began making videos on TikTok at the same time. Since then, he has amassed millions of followers from across the globe.

Rafa H. Arteaga is a Spanish-French product and fashion photographer based in Madrid. After finishing his studies in design, he started his career in photography. His work is inspired by the organic and timeless beauty of nature and the infinite possibilities of light. A work in continuous progress and exploration striving for a seamless connection between the photographic medium and the subject. The intention of his work in this book is the creation of a conversation between botany and the alteration of it by the hand of an artist.

INDEX